10P

The Haven of the Heart

PATIENCE STRONG

The Haven
of the Heart

I never cease to find it strange —
how in a flash the world can
change . . . Things can happen
overnight — and suddenly it all
comes right.

Life may not go the way you
planned. You cannot hope to
understand — the hidden hand
of Providence — that works
unseen behind events — but
patience waits to serve her turn
— and if on faith you lean, you
learn — to live by truths not
understood — that lead at last
unto the good — that you have
sought unconsciously; the haven
where your heart would be.

Birches
in November

Bare as bone against the skies —
the branches of the birches rise
— with their lean and leafless
forms — stripped to meet the
Winter storms.

Now their beauty I can see, silver
streaked with ebony — The pale
bark shimmers pearly white —
caught in lustrous loops of light.
Sentient they seem to be —
Awake, aware, alive to me. I did
not know. How could I guess —
that Summer hid such loveliness?

The Peace
that Heals

In these days of strife and
turmoil and perplexity — We all
need peace; the peace that heals
the mind — the peace that brings
the inward calm of quiet
thoughts, the previous balm —
that comes to us from worlds we
cannot see.

In these days of deep unrest we
need to seek a place — where we
at times can find a sanctuary —
discovering the joy that springs
from good and quiet and lovely
things — and learn the secret of
tranquillity.

The Companion

Don't depend entirely upon human consolations. Cultivate a quiet state of mind — where in spite of all your troubles, trials and tribulations — peace and satisfaction you will find.

There is One, the Good Companion, whom your heart is seeking — unconsciously you crave His company — In a crowd you miss the voice that unto you is speaking — saying, lonely child . . . Come unto Me.

There You Are

There you are again, I'm glad to see you here
once more — snowdrop swaying in the wind
outside my kitchen door . . . I knew you
wouldn't let me down or keep me waiting
long.

There you are on time to hear the blackbird
sing the song — that lifts the heart and fills
it full with thoughts of gratitude — for
beauty resurrected, faith confirmed and
hope renewed.

Would You Believe It?

Would you believe it? It's happened again —
the gold hazel catkins are out in the lane.
The crocuses making bright lakes in the
grass — ripple like waves as the stormy
winds pass.

The chiffchaff is building. The aconites glow
— like stars in the woods where the swelling
brooks flow. The winter is passing. I sense
on the breeze — the stirring of life in the
roots of the trees . . . The daffodils eager to
dance into view — are poised and are ready,
awaiting their cue. The spirit of Springtime
has tapped on the pane. Would you believe
it? It's happened again.

The Key Word

Do not think that happiness
resides in just what you possess.
Seek that happiness within —
and every morning will begin —
with thoughts of joy and
gratitude — Cultivate the
attitude — that life is sweet and
life is good — if God's great laws
are understood.

Do not say you cannot see — the
glimpses of divinity — behind the
drab and commonplace — you
feel the everlasting grace — but
only with your inner sight — can
you perceive this hidden light;
this aura, making dull things
shine — with splendour from a
source benign.

In the crowds that throng the
street — a radiant face you
seldom meet — so marked they
are with lines of care. A sunny
countenance is rare . . . The
world with all its sham and show
— can't tell you what you long to
know: the key word that will heal
and bless . . . The secret of true
happiness.

Escape From Yourself and be Free

Are you afraid of the shadows
that darken the path that you
tread — the fears and the doubts
that beset you when wondering
what lies ahead? . . . Remember
they're nothing but shadows and
shadows are cast by the light —
so cling to the hope that is in you,
then all will be well and come
right.

When thoughts of despair and
self-pity like shadowy ghosts
haunt the mind — you live in
perpetual twilight — no glimmer
of pleasure you find. Walk
straight through the cobwebs of
worry. Just brush them aside and
you'll see — the things that you
feared were but phantoms . . .
Escape from yourself and be free.

Troubles
Never Last

Don't assume that life will be all
May days. Make a plan for
coping with the grey days — so
that when they come — as come
they will, you will be prepared.
You'll know the drill. Have a
grey day programme all worked
out. Smile up at the cloud and
never doubt — that behind the
smoky murky smear — there's
glory . . . All is sunshine. All is
clear.

This remember always. Don't be
caught — off your guard. Be
ready with a thought — that
warms the heart. Though skies be
overcast — Troubles, like bad
weather, never last.

Go
With the Flow

Go with the flow of Providence
wherever that may be. Go with
the current that knows its way
into the open sea . . . Don't stand
about on the brink of life afraid
to venture in. Go with the flow of
circumstances. Follow the voice
within.

Go where God wills although it
leads to stress and turbulence —
Go with the driving of the wind
that moves the day's events . . .
Go where you're driven. Trust the
hand that will not let you go —
pulled by the tides, you know not
where, but going with the flow.

If the Heart is Singing

If the heart is singing you cannot go far
wrong — for you will discover there's magic
in a song — that scares away the demons
that throng around us all — wanting us to
stumble and to see us fall.

If the heart is singing nothing can get
through — only that which strengthens and
what is best for you.

Let the world go grumbling and grinding on
its way — for you'll have the secret that
lights the common day. You'll see the hidden
glory behind the leaden cloud. Lightly you
will travel, head high and back unbowed, for
when the heart is singing the soul is singing
too — Your sins will be forgiven, for every
day is new.

Together Again

Now we're together once more,
we two. The past we will bury
and start anew — making the
best of what years remain —
mending our marriage, beginning
again.

Wiser for every mistake we made
— letting unhappy memories
fade — thankful for having this
second chance — to pick up the
threads of the old romance.

Forward we'll look to the days
ahead — forgetting the things we
did and said. So foolish! Now
everything's marvellous. The
future is ours and it's up to us.

It's Catching

The mood of the blackbird that
trills in the tree — is gay; and I
feel it is trilling for me. The
mood of the skylark's ecstatic
delight — I feel in my blood as I
follow its flight . . .It's catching.

It may not be lasting, this tremor
of bliss — but is there a
happiness greater than this?

It touches the spirit, this note in
the air. This music, this magic
that banishes care . . . It's
catching.

The joy is infectious. I've caught
it, this thing that leaps in the
heart when the voices of spring
— carry the message that life is
renewed. This beautiful,
marvellous, wonderful mood — is
catching.

The Sun Breaks Through

Take comfort from the rhythm of
the seasons. It's Winter, but the
Spring will come again — as soon
as we have turned the Christmas
corner — come little signs that
Winter's on the wane.

You notice that the twilights
linger longer — And so in Life.
When trouble comes to you — it
never lasts. The dark cloud
passes over. Things change. Your
spirits rise. The sun breaks
through.

The Salt of the Earth

Somebody somewhere gave someone a smile.
Someone helped somebody over a stile . . .
Someone for somebody prayed in the night
— Someone was comforted; something came
right.

Somebody laughed when a quarrel seemed
near — Someone kept silence and fought
back the tear . . . These are the people who
do what they can — to lighten and brighten
this brief human span . . . Unknown and
unnoticed their small part they play —
making life bearable. Little they say — but
these are the great ones who fight the good
fight — the salt of the earth and the children
of light.

Let Love Speak

Let the word of peace be spoken — when
relationships are broken. Let Love speak and
heal the smart — of wounds inflicted on the heart.

Let Love's language, sweet and tender — its
own gentle service render — saying what is
kind and wise — with the lips or with the eyes.

Let no grievance leave an ember — that
perhaps you may remember — and regret in
later years — with your penitential tears.

Try forgiving. Try confessing. Let Love speak
the final blessing — casting every doubt away
— before the closing of the day.